Gym for the Brain

300 Riddles for Adults to Work out Their Mind Using Reason and Lateral Thinking

Karen J. Bun

Bluesource And Friends

This book is brought to you by Bluesource And Friends, a happy book publishing company.

Our motto is **"Happiness Within Pages"**

We promise to deliver amazing value to readers with our books.

We also appreciate honest book reviews from our readers.

Connect with us on our Facebook page www.facebook.com/bluesourceandfriends and stay tuned to our latest book promotions and free giveaways.

Don't forget to claim your FREE books!

Brain Teasers:

https://tinyurl.com/karenbrainteasers

Harry Potter Trivia:

https://tinyurl.com/wizardworldtrivia

Sherlock Puzzle Book (Volume 2)

https://tinyurl.com/Sherlockpuzzlebook2

Also check out our other books

"67 Lateral Thinking Puzzles"

https://tinyurl.com/thinkingandriddles

"Rookstorm Online Saga"

https://tinyurl.com/rookstorm

"Korman's Prayer"

https://tinyurl.com/kormanprayer

"The Convergence"

https://tinyurl.com/bloodcavefiction

"The Hardest Sudokos In Existence (Ranked As The Hardest Sudoku Collection Available In The Western World)"

https://tinyurl.com/MasakiSudoku

Description

This book is perfect for any adult, because we are giving you the power to shape and sharpen your mind to its best ability. With this book, you'll be able to exercise your brain and develop its functions that will allow you to live your best life. With these 300 puzzles and riddles, you can improve your memory and the sharpness of your brain while also having fun.

We all want our bodies to be at their best, and we work hard to get the body we want. But what about developing the mental abilities that we want? In our quest for our best life, we tend to neglect the mind. The mind needs our attention and care, too, but that doesn't have to be boring, and we don't have to shy away from the fun!

No one wants to be forgetful when they get older, or have to worry about not being able to think the way that they want to and the way that they are used to. When you have children, you want to be able to keep up with them and their thinking, and you don't want to feel as if you are being left behind. That's where this book comes in.

Riddles have been proven to have a great impact on your brain and how it works. It has also been proven that it can help you as you get older and that you can rewire your own brain to work better. In this book, the 300 riddles range from medium to extremely hard, and they are perfect for any adult on any level because, even if you're just starting out with riddles, we have riddles that you should be able to solve easily and have fun doing it. We start at a medium level, and then progress to the harder riddles once you've gotten the hang of it. You will be able to see that this book is innovative and creative, while being just what you need.

The riddles and puzzles are mixed, so you will be able to see easier ones mixed in with riddles that are more complicated. This way, you will not fall into boredom, and you can be kept on your toes. This is a fun and smart way to pass your valuable time. Another bonus of this book is that it's perfect for sharing with family members or your spouse. Have fun challenging each other to see who is able to determine the answer more quickly! It can even be a fun date night for couples who just want a night in!

The riddles and puzzles in this book are both challenging and fun, and we have interesting subjects that span many different cultures and accommodate many different thought processes. When you buy this book, you are going to stimulate your senses and take your brain for a ride. If you are looking for a great way to challenge your mind and spend your time doing something worthwhile, then this is the perfect book for you to read and enjoy anytime.

Introduction

Everyone has heard of a brain teaser at one point, and now, they are one of the most popular exercises that you can do in your spare time, and they're good for your brain. When people realized that brain teasers are perfect for helping their memory, they began jumping on the bandwagon to improve their brain functions.

Many children were probably introduced to puzzles when they were younger, by an elementary school teacher as a form of what is known as "fun homework". Since then, these brain teasers have stuck with them as they grew older, making it a favorite hobby. The best part about these brain teasers is that they can last through the ages, and you can take advantage of the benefits that they can have on your mental ability.

If you practice often enough with brainteasers, puzzles, or riddles, you have the potential to rewire your brain and strengthen it. Brainteasers can benefit your mind because they're built for lateral thinking. The art of thinking laterally is a way to solve problems by being creative. This lets you have a different approach to a problem. This type of problem-solving, along with analytical problem-solving, encourages you to think vertically instead.

The difference between brain teasers and riddles is that a brain teaser is often short and only a paragraph long at most, but to get to the answer, you need to use your creative thinking skills. Our riddles, on the other hand, are designed to make you think a little bit longer and a little harder than a brain teaser. Both brain teasers and riddles are beneficial to you, and one is not necessarily better than the other—they're just different approaches to different types of thinking.

Brainteaser riddles, like the kind in this book, can also improve your cognitive functions. The brain is neuroplastic, which means that it can change or shift over time. It is widely believed that when you get older, your brain will age as well. This is a fact that frightens most people because, as time goes, the brain will be less able to function, affecting one's competency. Growing old doesn't have to be a thing to fear, however, because there are things that you can do to slow down the effects of this process on your brain.

One thing that people should remember is that humans can change situations and help the negativity stay at bay and to ensure that it doesn't happen. This is because the brain is susceptible to everything that it is exposed to daily, and we can manipulate it. Examples of this include work, music, and the people around us. Everything that we partake in our daily lives has the potential to change how our brain is being wired.

This is where those brain puzzles and riddles come in. A perfect example of this is when we're watching the television. When we watch our favorite shows, our focus is on the show, and we are not really paying attention to what is going on around us. You can still learn from television, but most of the time, people watch television as a way to space out and not have to worry or think about anything that has happened throughout the day. In this case, you're not getting much from it.

A brain teaser, however, requires you to do some serious thinking to arrive at the right answer, which means that you are actually absorbing what you are doing, and you are paying attention to the task at hand. More importantly, you are actively involved in what you're doing.

Another benefit of solving riddles regularly is that it exercises our brain, allowing us to develop interpersonal skills or improve them as we get older. If you're solving something like a puzzle, then your brain would produce dopamine, which is essential for learning. Riddles can trigger our brain into forming a number of neural connections to find solutions for the questions thrown at us.

Thinking is one of the top mental activities that can bring us information and help us find a meaningful solution. This is one of the main reasons that solving riddles can help us improve our brain functions. Therefore, we should be doing them on a daily basis.

Chapter One: 300 Medium-to-Extremely Hard Riddles

1. What is one time that a man can have an empty coat pocket, but have something in it at the same time?
2. What has both wheels and flies but is not an aircraft?
3. There are two of us, and we are sisters.We are on different sides of a road, but we are unable to view each other. Can you tell what we are?
4. Can you deduce what has a corkscrew on one side and a power socket on the other?
5. Who buys this but has no use for it, makes it but doesn't need it, and uses it but can't feel it or see it? What is the item?
6. When I am in the first stages of my life, I am taller than I will be than when I am in my last stages. Can you deduce what I am?
7. If you dropped me from a tall building, I would be fine. If you put me in the water, I would die. What am I?
8. What type of room has no windows or doors?
9. What can you feed to make it live, but give it a drink and it will die?

10. A prisoner was told, "If you tell the truth, I am going to shoot you; if you tell a lie, I am going to stab you." What should the prisoner say to save his life?

11. I have water, but no fish live in it. I have mountains, but with no trees to speak of. I have towns, but I have no homes. Do you see what it is that I am?

12. I am in the middle of April and March, but I am not at the beginning or end of either month. What am I?

13. I am surrounded by wood, but I came from a mine. Everyone always uses me. What am I?

14. What is something that belongs to you that everyone else uses?

15. Think of what snow looks like, then think of what clouds look like. Before you think of anything else, what does a cow drink?

16. How is the number seven different from the other numbers between one and ten?

17. You eat me first, but then you get eaten. Can you deduce what I am?

18. What will always be in a minute and twice in a moment, but it will not be present in a thousand years?

19. How is it possible to have you stand physically behind your mother, while she is standing behind you as well?

20. I run, and it runs. When I stop, it still runs. What is it that I am speaking of?

21. The eyes will harvest, but the hand will sow.

22. The first will appear higher, while the second is wet. The whole can be something that ties, but there is also a writer's cramp.

23. I have left my campsite, and I hiked south, then east. I continue to the north for 3 miles each time, exactly. When I came back to my campsite, I saw a bear. What color is it?

24. If I have at least one daughter, I have less than ten daughters, or I have more than ten daughters. Only one of these statements is true. How many do I really have?

25. Some say I am green; some say I am red or yellow. Some play with what we are,and others spray us instead. What is it that we are?

26. You use me to stop, but you can take me to smoke. I stop, and I am a stop. I am the pool's first stroke. What am I?

27. What would be the most romantic part of the ocean?

28. A man found a photograph. His friend joins him and asks who is in it. The first man explains that he has no siblings, but in the photo, the man's parent is his parent's son.Can you deduce who it is in the photo?

29. A woman was standing at the side of a river. Her cat is on the other. She calls to the pet, and the pet crosses. Not a single drop of water has touched the pet, and there were no devices in place to help the cat cross. How did her cat manage the task?

30. Can you determine which is the odd one out? Snap, letter, mood, or stun?

31. If a sundial has the least amount of moving parts of any timepiece, what has the most?

32. What word has five letters but will become smaller if you add a duo of letters to it?

33. If your parents have six sons and you are one of them, and each son has one sister, how many people are in your family?

34. You have a class of students. Fourteen of the students are boys. Eight of the students wear blue shirts. Two of the students are neither male, nor wearing a blue shirt. If five of the children are boys who wear a blue shirt, then how many children would be in the class?

35. If Paul has a height of nine feet, and he works in a butcher shop while wearing size-twelve shoes, what would he weigh?

36. What has no legs, is brown, and has a head and tail?

37. If a monkey and a squirrel are both climbing at the same time, which one will reach the banana first?

38. What is something that will cease to have its head every morning, but will be able to have it again when nightfall arrives?

39. You have one jug of milk, and you need to measure a single cup. How can you achieve this if you only have a three-cup measuring container and a five-cup container?

40. If two fathers go fishing with their two sons, and they each catch a fish, why did they only bring home three fish?

41. I was a stone inside the tree; I help your words live. If you push me when I stand, I will have less, the more that I move around. Can you deduce what I am?

42. There is light, and it's the only place I can live. If light shines on me, however, I will die.

43. What sits when it stands up and jumps when it walks?

44. What has to be broken before you can use it?

45. What begins and ends with a T and has T inside it?

46. What is something that you can hold without using your arms?

47. It has been around for years, but it is never older than a month. What is it?

48. What has a single thumb, four fingers, but is not alive?

49. Three doctors said that James was their brother. James himself has said he has no brothers. Is James lying, or is the doctor lying?

50. If you remove the first and second from me and then remove all of the others, I will still be unchanged. Can you deduce what it is that I am?

51. I am a box that has no locks but holds keys. My keys have the power to unlock your deepest senses. What am I?

52. What has a single eye but is unable to see?

53. A woman in a hotel room is startled by a knock on the door. When she opens it, a man apologizes and explains that he thought it was his own room. When he leaves, the woman instantly locks the door and phones hotel security. Why was she so frightened of the man?

54. I have the ability to fly, but I do not have wings. I am able to weep; however, I do not have what is necessary

to see. The dark will always follow me, no matter where I go. Can you deduce what I am?

55. I am often bought for consumption, but no one will ever consume me. Can you guess what I am?

56. I am hard at the beginning and soft in the middle, and if you use me to blow, you will need to have a good amount of air. What am I?

57. Mr. Owens was killed on a Friday afternoon. His wife said she was reading a magazine and was innocent. The chef claimed that he was making breakfast and was innocent, as well. The maid had been folding clothes, and the butler was taking a shower as his mother was helping the gardener plant carrots in the garden. Who killed Mr. Owens?

58. What is a seven-letter word that becomes a one when you remove four?

59. I've been all around the world, and yet I never leave the corner. What am I?

60. What is something that you have that, the more you make, the more you leave behind?

61. What is something that breaks as soon as you speak its name?

62. A King has no heirs and no Queen, and he holds a contest to see who his heir will be. He gives each child

of the kingdom a seed and promises that whichever child has the largest and most beautiful plant will earn the throne. It's a metaphor for his kingdom. At the end of the contest, each of the children came back to the palace with an enormous and beautiful plant in their hand, each expecting to be the next ruler. He looks at all the children's plants, but finally decides that a little girl who has an empty pot is going to be the next Queen of the kingdom. If he had promised that the one with the most beautiful plant would win, why did he choose the little girl over all of the other children who had plants that grew?

63. At a funeral for her mother, a woman met a man she had never seen before. Upon seeing the man, she immediately fell in love at first sight. When the funeral is over, she tried to find him, but couldn't. Several days after the funeral, she killed her sister. Why would she kill her sister?

64. What is the type of dress that you were never able to wear?

65. What would you find at the end of a rainbow?

66. If you have this and then share it with other people, it's instantly gone. What is it?

67. If you open me, you cannot see me without the use of a mirror. If you close me, you will not be able to see me at all. What am I?

68. What type of tree can you carry in your hand?

69. What is something that rich people need, poor people have, and if you eat it, you die?

70. I am able to be cracked, and I am able to be made. You can play me, or you can tell me. What am I?

71. If I am something that is always being responded to, though I never speak with a question, what am I?

72. I have hands, but I am unable to clap. What am I?

73. I am present in the sun, but I am not in the rain. I have one color but more than one size. I can fly, though I am stuck at the bottom. I feel no pain and do no harm. What am I?

74. I do not have breath, but I am alive. I am always drinking but never thirsty. What am I?

75. I close one eye, though you beg me to keep it open. I have three eyes in total but only one leg. What am I?

76. What is a word in English that has nine letters but can remain a word at each step when you remove one letter from it, even to the point of a single letter remaining? You should list each letter as you are

removing them, and you should list the resulting word at each step you make.

77. I am always present in eternity, the final part of the time. I am at the start of the end and also of place. What am I?

78. Until you measure me, you will not know me. You will miss me when you cannot have any more of me. When I fly away, you will be saddened. What am I?

79. I have four legs, but I am not able to walk. I am covered in flowers on a special occasion, but I have no soil for them to grow. I hold food many times throughout the day, both large and small. What am I?

80. I hurt the most when I am lost, but I hurt when I'm not had at all. In some cases, I am the hardest to express, but I can also be the easiest that you find to ignore. I am something that can be given to many or just one. Can you deduce what I am?

81. The fighters are lined up and placed with gratification. There is a duo of lines that will stand alongside each other. A single component will be able to deduce whether the other rows are going to be divided or united. What is the thing that we are talking about?

82. I cannot breathe, but I can jump and skip. I am able to run great distances, but I cannot eat. I can stretch,

and I can swim over vast lakes, but I do not drink. I can stand, and I can fall asleep. I can play, and I can grow, but I do not think or have a mind of my own. You see me, but I cannot see at all. What am I?

83. Within me, I am able to clean all that is old and what is bad. The juice that I make is golden. If I die, you will need to assemble a filter machine to replace me and the beans that I resemble. What do you think I am?

84. Two politicians sit at a table and discuss business. They each order the same drink. One politician, named Tommy, drinks his right away and orders another. He drinks his second in a gulp, but decides to wait before he orders another. The other politician, named Tony, sips his drink but suddenly falls forward and dies. Both men were set up to be assassinated. Why, then, did Tony die, and why did Tommy live?

85. I am never fat, but I can be very thin. You always need me around, but I never crowd you, and I give you your space. You can use a lot of me, especially if you like to talk. I am always around for you, but the ability to view me will not happen. What am I?

86. I am a danger to everyone, and I am a true cause for you to be alarmed. If you see me, you could lose your

life, your home, or those that are precious to you. When you hear me, you could lose your job in an instant. What am I?

87. If I order a sword that is priced at $400, but I live in an area where I cannot have a package longer than 9 feet, and my sword is 9 feet and 1 inches, how would it be mailed to me without breaking the rules of the country that I am in? I would like my sword to arrive in one piece.

88. Duels are of evil and good, but I am a fighter of good. If you watched your words, I would be revealed. I am considered to be a king of the night sky that is black. What am I?

89. I can take you up, or I can take you down. You can reach great heights with me, or you can be at the bottom. What am I?

90. I am old, and I have been around for ages. I have a mighty roar. I am able to run forever, though I never move at all. What am I?

91. You're supposed to keep me as straight as possible, though you can very rarely do so. For much of the time, I am curved or slightly bent, and your sadness or depression can cause me to bend even further. If you keep bending me over and over again, or if you bend

me for too long, you may find that I am unable to straighten out again. What am I?

92. I can be dull, or I can shine brightly. I am many different sizes. I can be large in size, and I can also be small. I can be curved, or I can be pointy. I can be sharp, or I can be unsharpened. You see me every day, but it is only when you need me that I become apparent in your mind. What am I?

93. I am visited by people every day from all over the world. They can come and visit me because I stay in one place. Some stay with me for a few minutes, although some stay with me for an hour. Most of the people who meet me think that I am dirty, but they never want to be without me because they need me around. Whenever people come to see me, they open themselves up and reveal a part of themselves that they don't show to other people. Who or what am I?

94. There was a driver for a businessman who was going the wrong way down a street that was one way. On his way, he passes 7 police officers who watch him go the wrong way down a one-way street, yet none of them make a move to stop him, or even speak to him angrily. Instead, they smiled, waved, and wished him well. Why did none of the 7 police officers stop him?

95. A ruler of a kingdom has a wine bottle supply that is the number equivalent to a hundred and ten products. One bottle has been filled with poison. One single taste of the wine with poison is enough to kill a person. Not wanting to be poisoned himself, the king asks the jailer to identify the poisoned wine by testing them on prisoners. It takes a full day for the poison to take effect. The dungeons have been filled, so he can test it on as many prisoners as he needs to. What is the minimum number of prisoners who have to be tested with the wine?

96. Many people can perceive me, though no one experiences the joy of being able to view me. When you speak to me, I will respond, but only if you make the first move. What am I?

97. A cleaner of windows is high above the ground, placed at the 12th level at a hotel. Upon stumbling, he begins to tumble downward. Though there is no equipment to prevent dangerous activity, he is fine. This is impressive, but how did it happen?

98. I'm only made for one person, but my purpose is for two. I can be worn for many years, but sadly, I'm usually only worn for a few. You're supposed to keep

me on forever, but that isn't always the case. You will never need me unless you say that you do. What am I?

99. I get used every day, whether a lot or a little, although you are kind enough to let me rest at night. I have a twin with me at all times, and I'm never alone. For some reason, you always cover me up instead of letting me go. I am not alive, but I do have a soul, and so does my twin. What am I?

100. You are sitting at a table, trying to enjoy your dinner, and you notice that there are 22 flies on your table. You begin swatting right away, and you are able to kill 10 flies. How many flies are there left on the table after you killed 10?

101. A student has missed more school than any other student, and the principal has called him into his office and asked him why he's missing so many school days. The student angrily replies that there isn't enough time for him to attend because he needs a certain length of sleep every day, and he calculates that he would need 122 days of sleep. After calculating, weekends count for over 100 days in the year and summer vacation is 2 months. He also declares that if he spent an hour on each meal, that would accumulate to 45 days in a year. He further

calculates that he would need at least 2 hours to relax and to do whatever he wanted to do in a day, which adds another month to his schedule. He then says that if you add all of that, it would only leave him 4 days for school. The principal is confused and rightly so, but he is unable to figure out why. What is wrong with the student's argument to confuse the principal?

102.   There was once a king who had 3 wise men, and he told them that they must close their eyes. When their eyes are closed, he goes around and put a glove on each one of them. "I have put a red or yellow glove on each of you," he says to them. "I will not tell you what color the glove is, but one of you has the red one." "Open your eyes," he commands. "You may not speak to each other at all, but within a single hour, I want one of you to call out the color of your glove. If you are unable to do this, or if one of you says the wrong color, you will all be exiled from my kingdom immediately." Instantly, they began to look at each other's gloves. After standing for the entire hour in silence, all three men figure out the color of their gloves and speak at once. If you're assuming that all of these men and the others have perfect logic and they are all able to think at the same time with the same

speed to figure out who had what color, what then are the colors of the 3 men's gloves?

103.　　　An offense had occurred on Baker avenue. Police thought that a man, Kyle Ferguson, was to blame. They believed that someone running on a pathway was suddenly stabbed in the chest. The suspect had brown hair with bright blue eyes, and he wore the same suit that Kyle Ferguson was wearing. The suit that he was wearing was a Gucci suit. When questioned about his involvement in the crime, Kyle said that he was innocent, and that he was walking through the pathway when someone who was wearing a suit just like his came up behind the victim and stabbed the victim. He claimed he was scared and ran home as quickly as his feet would take him so that his own life would not be taken as well. When the police asked him to give a description of the murderer, he repeated that he had the same suit on as the one he was wearing, but the other man had bushy black hair, a full beard, and a baggy and torn suit. Instantly, the policeman knew that Kyle was lying. How was it possible that they were able to tell that Kyle wasn't telling the truth?

104.   Mrs. Benson teaches 2nd-grade students. One
of the attendees decided to take the apple that was
sitting on her desk. To figure out who had done it,
Mrs. Benson had narrowed the suspects down to:
Paige, Bonnie, and Heather. Each of the students gave
the same statement, except for one. Both Paige and
Bonnie said that they didn't do it. Only Heather
blamed someone else, and she said that Bonnie didn't
do it either. She knows that only one of the children is
telling the truth, but who is telling the truth about
who took the apple?

105.   A woman puts on a clean shirt every night
before she goes to bed. On the first night, she puts on
a blue shirt and then sleeps for 5 hours. For every
hour more that she sleeps, she decides to put on a
different shirt. The next night, she follows a scale that
contains different colors. The colors are: Blue, black,
red, green, white, pink, orange, brown, purple, yellow,
gray, neon green, tan and, finally, teal. After she does
this, every hour less than the night before, she will put
on a different color, going backwards on the scale that
she has created. If she decides to wear a blue shirt, it
is because, she slept more hours than the night before.
She does this because if she had slept fewer hours

than the previous night, she would skip it and wear the teal shirt instead. However, if she continues to go backward on the scale, and she had to wear blue but would not wear it, she would still be counting blue from the scale, backward. The second night, the woman decides to wear a blue shirt because she hadn't slept any more or less hours than she had the previous night. The night that she wears a blue shirt, she sleeps for 6 hours. The night after, she sleeps for 5. On the 4th night, she sleeps for 8 hours, and on the next night, she sleeps for only 7 hours. The night after that, she is able to sleep well and sleeps for 11 hours. On night number 7, she stays up very late, and she only gets 4 hours of sleep. The following night, she's exhausted, so she sleeps for 14 hours and discovers that she is sick. Because she had slept so long the previous night, the next night she only sleeps for 7 hours. The night after, she is tired, so she sleeps for an hour more. On the night following that, she has done so much work that she was only able to sleep for 5 hours, but the night following this, her boss at work decided to let her out early, so she has more time to sleep. This enables her to sleep for an additional 4 hours. The night after that, she sleeps for a solid 8 hours. On the last night, the woman manages to get 10 hours of sleep, but then one more night follows, and she decides to put on a different colored shirt according to the scale that she had put in place. On the following night, she decides to pick a shirt randomly. On which night will the woman wear blue again?

106.   There is a kingdom with poison, and everyone knows that the only way that you can cure yourself is to drink an even stronger poison to neutralize the poison that you've already drunk. The king doesn't want to die and wishes to make the strongest poison possible so that, anytime he gets poisoned, the poison that he takes will neutralize any other poison that he has been given. In order to make sure that this can happen correctly, he ordered two chemists to come to his kingdom. They are the best chemists in the land, and have proven their value. Their names are: Stewart and Lenny. The king is going to have them both create a poison as strong as they can make it, and after they've completed their poison, he will then have others to drink them and then their own. Whoever dies has created the weaker poison. Stewart knows that Lenny is much better at making poison than he

is, so he knows that he is more likely to die. Using this knowledge, Stewart makes a plan to ensure that he will live, but that Lenny will die. On the day of the contest, Lenny realizes that Stewart knew that he had no chance of beating him, so Lenny quickly thinks of a plan that will ensure that he will live, and Stewart will die instead. In the end, Lenny is the one who lives, while Stewart is the one who dies. The king is left unhappy because he didn't get what he wanted. What happened?

107.   On a Friday night, you and your buddies are bored, so they have decided to give you a dare involving a house that is known to be haunted and dangerous. You walk up to the front door, and you're scared because you have no idea what's behind it. When you go in, you find a long hallway that leads into a musty room that has three separate doors. You try to turn back, but the doors close behind you and get locked. No one can hear you screaming for help, and the room is dark. You look for a light source and try to turn it on, but the power is out, so it doesn't work. You're terrified, but now, you have no choice but to follow the hallway to the three doors, and you must make a choice. Behind the first door is an

electric chair that you have to sit in. Behind the second door, there's a bottomless pit that has no end, and behind the last door, there's a pool full of acid. You have to go into one of the rooms, and you have to face the danger. Which of the three doors should you go through?

108.　　　You have a grandparent who is an inventor, and he has a pink and green tablet for you. Ingested together, they will grant you immortality. On the night he invented it, he gives you two of the pink pills and two of the green pills, just in case one of them is lost, or one of them doesn't work. As he's your grandfather and he loves you, he gives you a special warning: If you overdose, you will get the opposite, and you will die. You put the pills in your purse, and you leave and go home. Unfortunately, on the way home, you are abducted by kidnappers, and they blindfold you. They throw you in the back of their car. At this point, you remember the pills that your grandfather invented. You take them out because you have retained motion in your arms. You are only able to breathe for a few moments longer. The problem is, you cannot tell in the dark, which is the pink tablet and which is the green tablet. Unfortunately, even if you remove your blindfold, there are no lights, so you are unable to see. Given the circumstances that you're in, how can you successfully eat one tablet that's pink and one tablet that's green so that you can make sure that you survive?

109.   My stalk is placed securely wherever my presence is allowed. My back end appendage is curly. I mature to a part of my full height as you dot me. Not a single word can I speak, yet I can communicate in any dialect you wish. I'm not a seed, but birds love me. I have a speech impediment that affects me. I can say "aged", but I cannot say the word "wage"; I can say the word "cage", but I cannot say the word "page". I reside on the main road that is built well. You will be able to view my companions here as they are committed. I am well-constructed; however, I am not rotated, and I'm a tool for learning. To understand what I am, you must calculate me before you start. What am I?

110.   There is a small town that is known for having two barbershops. Each of these barbershops has only one hairstylist, and they reside in conflicting areas of the town. One area is well-known, and one is judged for its appearance. The hairstylist in the first part of the town is always clean, and the air is fresh. The

floors are always washed, and there's no hair on the floor. The barber is extremely friendly, and he is always smiling. Also, he is well put-together, and his hair is well-done. The stylist in the conflicting part of the town is not well put-together. The shop has filth. The stylist wears an unhappy face. His hair is not well-made at all, and you can see stains and tears on his shirt. His skin is oily, indicating that he's not able to wash his face. Newcomers come to the town and hear about both stylists, and get information about both. After doing so, they decide to visit the second stylist with the bad hair, instead of the first. Why would they do this?

111.　　　　　There is a circular jail that has a single warden. He is extremely hyper one day; he runs around and begins to open cells. They have 100 cells in this jail, and they are numbered from 1 to 100. Running in a circle and opening all the cells, he quickly runs around and begins to close every second cell starting with 2. So the sequence would go 2, 4, 6, 8, 10, 12, and so on. If a cell is open, he closes it, and if a cell is closed, he opens it. When he finishes running by all of the cells in the jail, he opens and closes every third cell. This sequence would be 3, 6, 9, 12, 15, 18, and so on, then every fourth cell starting with 4. This makes the sequence 4, 8, 12, 16, 20, and so on. He does this until he goes around and only changes the 100th cell, which is the last cell. When he is done with all of this, which cells are actually still open?

112.   A bank is being robbed, and one of the robbers says to one of the bank tellers that she has to give him all of the money. But their bank teller explains to him that she doesn't have access to it. After she's done speaking, the phone rings, and the robber tells her to answer it and that she better not give them away, or he will kill her. When she picks up the phone, she realizes it's her mother. She asks her mother if this was an emergency situation. Then she asks her mother if she could please call her once she gets home. She then states she needs help painting before she hangs up the phone. The robbers continue to try and get into the vaults but without success. Twenty minutes later, the police show up with the teller's mother and arrests all of the robbers who are in the bank. How did the police know about the robbery?

113.   A man named Adam has three daughters who are unmarried. The oldest daughter always tells the truth, while the youngest daughter always lies. The

middle child either tells the truth or lies. One day, a very rich and handsome young man comes to Adam's house and says that he wants to marry one of his daughters. Naturally, he wants to marry the oldest or the youngest so that he will always be able to tell if she is lying or telling the truth to him. Their father agrees and understands the reasoning behind his logic, but he says that he will only allow him to ask one of the girls a question, and it has to be a yes or no question. Once he does this, he can decide which one he is going to marry. Unfortunately for the handsome man, all of the daughters look the same age. What question would he ask one of the daughters at random to be able to figure out which daughter is the youngest or the oldest, so he knows which daughter tells the truth or which one lies?

114.   You are visiting your best friend who tells about a tale of how he attempted to impress a beautiful young woman with a story, but instead got slapped across his mouth. He wants you to see why he got slapped, because he doesn't understand. His story is as follows. "On a hot and windless day, we were in a bunker, and one of us yelled that the enemy is coming. We immediately began to open fire and defended our

bunker, leaving 100 men dead before they were able to retreat. I was checking out a dead captain's glasses when a shout came that more men were coming, and the captain ordered us to open fire with our mortars. I yelled for ceasefire immediately, realizing that they were Americans after I had seen their flag-waving back and forth. Later, a colonel, who was American, thanked me for it." What is wrong with this story?

115. Tristan's teacher asked him: If she gave him 2 cats and then 2 more and 2 more after that, how many would he have? Right away, Tristan said, "7." His teacher then asked him, more slowly, that if she gave him 2 cats, then 2 more and 2 more, how many would he have? Again, he gave her the same answer, and again, she asked him the same question. He replies, "6." Happy that he seemed to understand what was going on, she asks him one more time that if she gave him 2 cats, and then 2 more and 2 more, how many would he have? Thinking for a second, he replied again, "7" and seemed upset that the teacher couldn't understand where his math was coming from. Johnny is not wrong, and his teacher is wrong, but why?

116. Ben was the most powerful man on the globe, and he had the skill to lift something that weighed

1,000 kg easily. He even boasted that he was able to pick up 5 women at once without feeling a single ounce of pain. One day, there was a weightlifting show that was well known, so the top 5 strongest men entered, including Ben. The challenge was that they were going to have to lift up an extremely heavy object of 1,005 kg for 5 minutes. Whoever didn't drop it until the target time would be the winner. If everyone did it, the judges would decide to give first place to the person who lifted it the most easily and stood still without any trouble at all. If Ben was the strongest, then he would have come out first, but instead, when the challenge was over, he placed second. Why did he place second and not first?

117.   There was a woman who wanted to treat her aunt from an illness, so they went to the doctor. The doctor told her that she would need to eat a single apple in order to cure her aunt. In the village where they were staying, no one had any apples, so she tried another village. When she got there, she realized that they had millions of apples in a garden, but when she tried to get in, the gatekeeper told her that all the apples that she brings out of the garden should be shared between them. So how many apples did the

woman come out with from the garden to share with the gatekeeper while keeping an apple to cure her aunt?

118.   There were 4 men who walked to a desert. All 4 men are knocked out at the same time, and when they awaken, their bodies are buried in the sand. They cannot look anywhere but straight ahead of them. They were positioned in a way that each man can see another man's head before them. However, between the first and second man, there's a wall. Because of this, the only thing the first man can see is the desert, and the only thing the second man can see is the wall. The third man sees the second man's head and the wall, and the fourth man sees 2 heads and the wall. On top of each man's head is a hat; the underside of each hat is pink, but the outside of each hat is either of green or red. Before any of the men can speak, their kidnappers have told them that if they speak, they will die. If one of them can guess the color of their hat on the first try, then they get to live, and they can go free. The kidnappers have told them that there are 2 green hats and 2 red hats. Because we are smart, and we can observe the situation, we can deduce that the order of the hats is green then red and green then red again.

We know the perspective that each man has and that they can only see the desert, the wall, or the color of the cap in front of them. Out of the 4 men, who knows for sure the color of his own hat, and more importantly, why does he know the color of his own hat?

119.   A prison has 23 prisoners and 23 cells, so each prisoner is alone in their cell. The prisoners have no way to communicate with each other in any way. There is another room, though. They have a rec room. The rec room has 2 switches on the wall: An A switch and a B switch. The switches have both on and off positions, but they start in an unknown position. The prisoners are randomly taken to and from the rec room one at a time, and they must change the position of only one of the 2 switches every time they go into that room. At any point, a prisoner can yell out that every prisoner has been here. If the prisoner is correct that all of the prisoners have visited that room, they can all go free. If they were wrong, then they are all executed instead. Before they start, they are given one session to plan, during which they can discuss a method to understand how to win the game. What

method could they use to make sure that they all go free instead of being executed?

120.　　　You have been kidnapped and poisoned by a scientist who is pure evil. He has told you that the only antidote is the saliva of a lizard. He has the saliva of 6 different animals: An iguana, a lizard, a koala, a lemur, a giraffe, and a cow. He hasn't labeled the test tubes, so you have no way of knowing who is and what is what. On the left is a table where 4 of the test tubes are residing, and on the right, 2 test tubes are residing. The lizard saliva is what can save you, and the iguana is poisonous. The test tubes of the lizard and the iguana are on the same table. The table that has tubes on the left are labeled 1, 2, 3, and 4. The lizard saliva will not override the iguana poison. The poison and the lizard saliva are not right beside each other. You don't know where the cow test tube is, but you know that the cow is in either number 2 or number 3. You know that the iguana test tube is not to the right of the cow. You only have time to drink 2 test tubes, so which side do you run toward, and which test tubes do you drink?

121.　　　There is a cell of 100 prisoners, and each prisoner is kept out of contact with the others. In one area of the prison, there is a single light bulb. Every day, the warden picks a prisoner at random; it doesn't matter if they have been picked before. If he picks you, you will be taken to the lobby. The prisoner then has the choice to flip on the switch if they choose to do so. The light bulb will go off. When the prisoner is taken into the area with the lightbulb, he has the option of saying that every prisoner has been brought to the light bulb. If it's true, the prisoners go free, but if it's false, the prisoners die. A prisoner should only say this if he knows 100% that it's true. Before the first day of the process, all of the prisoners are allowed to get together to discuss a strategy that could possibly save themselves. What strategy should they use about the light bulb to ensure that they will go free?

122.   A husband and wife are in the emergency room because the wife is in labor. When they arrive, the doctor says that he invented the new machine that could transfer part of the mother's labor pain to the baby's father. He then asked the couple if they're willing to try it. They were both very much in favor of this idea, so the doctor set the pain transfer to 10% and explained that 10% was probably more pain than the father had experienced before. However, as the

labor progressed, the husband felt fine and asked the doctor to make it higher. The doctor adjusted the machine to 10% higher, and the husband was still feeling fine.The doctor checked the husband's blood pressure; he was amazed to see that he was doing amazingly well. At this point, they decided to try 50% of pain transfer. The husband continued to feel fine, and since the pain transfer was obviously helping the wife considerably, the husband encouraged the doctor to transfer every single ounce of pain to him instead of his wife. The wife delivered a healthy baby with no pain, and she and her husband were ecstatic. When they got home, they saw that their mailman was dead on the porch. Why did the mailman die instead of her husband?

123.   There isa quintet of homes that were painted in a quintet of different colors. In each dwelling lives a person with a different nationality. The 5 people also drink a certain type of beverage, and they smoke a particular brand of cigar. They all have a particular pet, and none of them have the same pet. None of them smoke the same brand of the cigars, and none of them drink the same beverage. If the man living in the center house drinks milk, while the green homeowner

drinks coffee, and the greenhouse is on the left of the white house, we can use these clues to determine who lives where. The British native lives in a red house, and the Dane drinks tea. The German only smokes Prince cigars, and the person who has Norwegian nationality lives next door to the blue house. The Norwegian lives in the first house and the owner of the yellow house only smokes Dunhill cigars. The Swede only keeps dogs as pets, and the man who only smokes Blend cigars has a neighbor who only drinks water. The owner of the house who only drinks beer smokes Blue master cigars. The person who smokes Pall Mall cigars only has birds, and the person who smokes the Blend cigars lives next to the owner who keeps the cats. The man who keeps the horse lives next to the man who smokes the Dunhill cigars. Keeping all of this in mind, who owns the fish?

124.   Brandon went camping and realized he forgot his sleeping bag. He goes to get it, comes back, and realizes he forgot his flashlight. Brandon goes and gets it, but when he comes back, he finds that his sleeping bag is missing. Brandon then finds out he forgot his tent. When he goes back and gets it, he sees his sleeping bag, grabs it, and leaves his tent. He goes

back to the campsite, remembering he left his tent at home. Brandon also finds out his flashlight is now missing. He goes to get his tent and see his flashlight and grabs that too. Brandon then sees his sleeping bag is gone. He is so exhausted; he leaves it at home. Why does everything keep going missing?

125.   Two guys go to get a drink. One gentleman has a baseball cap, and the other, a cowboy hat. The one with the baseball cap walks up the bar and says, "If I can shoot beer out of this tube to a glass on the other side of the room, you have to give me a five hundred dollars. If I miss, I will give you five hundred dollars." The bartender agrees. The guy with the baseball cap puts down a glass and goes to the other side of the room. He shoots beer out of the tube but sprays it everywhere. The bartender laughs. However, the baseball cap guy is also laughing. The bartender asks, "Why are you laughing?" Why was the guy with the baseball cap laughing?

126.   There are four guys: Chris, Brad, Mike, and Josh. There is a quartet of headgear: Two white and two black. They each get a hat. Chris gets the black, Brad gets the white, Mike gets the black, and Josh gets the white. They don't know what hat color they have.

Chris goes into a room so that no one can see his hat. The others line up in front of the door in the order: Brad, Mike, and Josh (Brad can't see the other hats; Mike can see Brad's, and Josh can see Mike and Brad's hats). Whoever can figure out their hat color first wins $1,000. If they are wrong, they are out of the running. Which man can figure out his hat color without a doubt?

127.   There once was a gentleman who was the director of acaravan, and he ran someone over, so he got sentenced to death. When he goes to the electric chair, the people who work there told him that it was his last day to live, so what would he like to eat? He says that he wants peanut butter and cereal, and when they turn on the electric chair, they aresurprised that nothing happens. The next day, he gets sent to an electric chair that they boast is 10 times better than the one before. They asked him again what he would like to eat, and he says the same thing. He eats the same meal, and they turn on the electric chair once more, and nothing happens.The next day, he gets sent to Alcatraz, and they ask him the same question, and he says the same answer. When they turn on the electric chair, still nothing happens, so the next day,

they send him to the best electric chair in the entire world. They ask againwhat would he like to eat, and he answers the same as he had before. Once he eats the meal that he had eaten three times already, they turn on the electric chair, and nothing happens. Finally, they lose their patience and yell at him, demanding to know why he is not getting electrocuted, and the conductor replies with what?

128.   There is an island in which 201 inhabitants reside. Half have green eyes, while 100 have brown eyes, and the island leader has blue eyes. To leave the island, you have to know your own eye color. However, this is difficult because there are no reflective surfaces on the island, and no one can communicate with one another, other than the leader to the residents of the island. No one on the island knows how many of each eye color there is and everyone on the island is a perfect logician. This means that if there is a solution to be found, they will find it. Every morning, the leader gives everyone a chance to leave the island by guessing their eye color. One morning,the leader gathers all of the residents to make an announcement, and he says that one person on this island has green eyes. How many people are

able to leave the island, and in how many days after the announcement can they leave?

129.   I am the oldest child of my father; I can live without men, but men can't live without me. The next oldest child of my father has seen men rise and fall and have all of their secrets in his belly; the third child of my father can never give you his gift forever; he takes it from you when you corrupt it unknowingly, but men cry for his gift no matter what its cost is. The second youngest of my father is an obedient servant in the hands of men, but when he loses his master, he becomes an unmerciful god. The youngest child of my father is the center of our lives; he guides us, but he is a divine mystery. What are we?

130.   A man goes into a store and spends 15 dollars. He pays the manager with a 20 dollar bill, but the register doesn't have change because it is an especially slow day. The manager at the register goes to the thrift shop next to his own and trades the 20 dollar bill for a 10 dollar bill and two 5 dollar bills. Then he gives the man his 5-dollar change. Later, the woman from the thrift shop confronts the manager and tells him that the 20-dollar bill he gave her was counterfeit. The manager agrees, and he gives the lady a different 20-

dollar bill. Later that day, the manager tries to figure out how much money he lost. What did he lose?

131.   A woman is on trial for murdering her spouse. In the final words, the woman's lawyer surprises everyone when he announces, "Her husband was just missing. Everyone look at those doors; her husband is going to walk through those doors in about 30 seconds."The entire court is silent, and the jury stares at the door as the lawyer and the defendant stare at them. After a couple of minutes, the lawyer says, "See! If you were so sure she killed her husband, you wouldn't be watching that door!"The jury goes into deliberation and comes back almost immediately with a guilty verdict.Why did the jury convict her?

132.   One guy reveals that a prize of $1,000 will be given to whoever can prove that they deserve it. One woman posts (the post receives 1 point): Don't give it to me; others deserve it more. The next guy posts (this person also receives 1 point): If you give the money to me, I'll spend it to make this world a better place. The final guy posts a picture of a dog. His post gets -1 point. When posting, if somebody dislikes your comment, you lose a point, and when somebody likes

it, you gain a point. You can also vote on your own. Who gets the money?

133.　　　A guilty person is placed in jail for felony misdeeds. The man in charge tells him that he will be killed in the middle of the prison by 10 of his guards. The criminal is fine with that, but he asks for some conditions: "All of your men must stand 10 feet away from me, and I must be able to select where each guard stands. If I survive, I get to leave." The warden thinks about it and knows that all of his guards will still have an open shot at the criminal, so he agrees. The next day after the firing squad is positioned, the criminal walks out untouched. How did he do it?

134.　　　There is a wagon filled with headgear. A trio of them are orange, and a duo of them are red. There are 3 men: Jack, James, and Jim. They each take a hat out of the basket and put it on their heads without seeing the hat they selected or the hats the other men selected. The men arrange themselves, so Jack can see James and Jim's hats, James can see Jim's hat, and Jim can't see anyone's hat. Jack is asked what color his hat is, and he says he doesn't know. James is asked the same question, and he also doesn't know. Jim is asked the question, and he does know. What color is his hat?

135.   Four mountain bikers are placed in a building in complete darkness because of a bad lightning storm. On the door of the cabin is a paper that reads, "Come in as you please, but fall asleep, and you will die." Being very superstitious, they all take this very seriously and devise a plan so they can keep each other awake. They each stand in separate corners, and one person walks from one corner, along the wall to the next and taps the person in that corner, making sure they are awake. They do this for many hours until one mountain biker suddenly runs out of the cabin, screaming along with all of the others. Why did they run out terrified?

136.   Three guys, 1, 2, and 3, are spoken to. There is no sequence to how they were spoken to.Honest, Liar, and Both is one name they go by. The following are the others: True always speaks the truth, False always speaks lies, but whether Random speaks truth or lies in a completely random matter. Your task is to determine the identities of 1, 2, and 3 by asking three yes or no questions—each question must be put to exactly one guy. The guys understand English but will

answer all questions in their own language, in which the words for "yes" and "no" are "da" and "ja", in some order. You do not know which word means which. What three questions can you ask?

137.   A prince and princess want to have a get-together with friends whom they know, and with no strangers or sneak-ins. They decided to make a password to get into the party. On the day of the party, a man who wasn't invited wanted to get into the party, so he paid attention to what the people with the passwords were saying. Guard: "Pig" Person: "Farm" *next person* Guard: "Bear" Person: "Woods" *next person* Guard: "Frog" Person: "Water." The intruder thought he had the password, so when the guard said "Bird," the Intruder said "Tree." He was thrown out of the party. Why?What could have he used for the password?

138.   In a condo residents building in Los Angeles, there is a centuplicate of married couples. When one of the husbands cheats on his wife with one of the other wives, his wife has no idea.With a large amount of gossip in the complex, all of the other wives know he is cheating. If a wife finds out that her husband is cheating on her, she kills him the following morning.

Someone anonymously sends an email to all of the wives in the building, saying that at least 1 man is cheating on his wife in the building. How many husbands will be killed, and how long will it take?

139.   There are 100 criminals lining up to go to jail. Each criminal is wearing a shirt that is either black or white. The criminals don't know their own shirt color—just the shirt color of those in front of them in line (the first criminal in line can't see anyone's shirt, and the last criminal can see everyone's shirt except his own). Starting from the back, one of the guards asks each criminal what color their shirt is. If they are correct, they get to go free, but if they are wrong, they go to jail. If everyone gets to discuss a plan, how can at least 99 of them be saved?

140.   A man is sitting down in a bar alone. A woman walks in, and he notices right away that she's extremely rich. She sits down next to him, and he tells her that he has an amazing talent and that he knows almost every song that has ever existed. The woman laughs at him. The homeless man tells her that he is willing to bet all the money that she has in her wallet that he can sing a popular song that includes a title of her choosing. She laughs again; then she says she

wants him to sing a song about her daughter. Her daughter's name wasFrederica Armstrong Miller. The homeless man goes home rich. What song did he sing to the rich woman?

141.   If a man rode into town on Friday and came back on Friday, how did he do it?

142.   If an electric train is traveling south, which way will the smoke be going?

143.   What is always at the center of a woman but in front of a man?

144.   I can be crushed into pieces with words or by physical pain, but this only happens if I am given away first. I can be clogged, or I can be attacked, but that is usually my own doing and not someone else's. You won't dare ever let me go no matter how many problems I have; you'll keep me forever. What am I?

145.   I can jump around on sticks, and if you think I've done well, you'll cheer me when I do this. White powder is a necessity in my life to make sure that I can do what I need to do. When you look at me, you might wonder why I look like I'm always about to go swimming. What am I?

146.   I owna large space, but I also have a home. I have no locks, but I do have many keys. I have no mailbox, but I have a lot of letters. What am I?

147.   I have different nationalities, and I can be dark or white. I can be bitteror sweet. My nationality may be Swiss or Belgian. I even possess the ability to be other nationalities as well. What am I?

148.   I'm attracted to treats, and I'm attracted to sugars. I am small but hard-working, and I sound like I would be a member of your family. What am I?

149.   I have different nationalities. I can be Greek or Roman, English or Latin. I come in many different amounts, and I am unique in the fact that you can match me or mix me, and I can take on almost an infinite number of different forms. What am I?

150.   A quartetmust make it along a wire in just over 15 minutes, along with a duo of minutes added on. They must do this during the night. The wire can only hold two or fewer people at any time, and they only have one flashlight, so they must travel together (or alone). The flashlight can only travel with one person, so every time it crosses the bridge, it must be carried back. Jack can cross in 1 minute, Jason can cross in 2 minutes, Alex can cross in 5 minutes, and Cindy can

cross in 10 minutes. If two people cross together, they go as fast as the slower person. How can they cross the wire in 17 minutes or less?

151.   A woman taking a questionnaire approaches the home where a physicist resides. She questions if he has any kids, and how old they are. The physicist says, "I have three sons, and the product of their ages is 72." The woman tells the physicist that she needs more information, so the physicist tells her, "The sum of their ages is equal to our house number." The woman still needs more information, so the physicist tells her, "My oldest son has his own bed, and the other two share bunk beds." How old are his sons?

152.   A worker is employed for a network security company. He clocks in at night and gets on his computer. He types in his password, but it is incorrect. He remembers that the password changes every 2 weeks, so he calls his boss. The man says, "Boss, the old password is out of date." The boss replies, "Yes, the new password is different. But if you listen closely, you can figure it out. It has the same number of letters but no spaces." The man thanks the boss and types the password immediately. What is the new password and the old password?

153.   A CEO is about to take a trip to Scotland. He is awoken in the middle of the night by his bodyguard, John, the night before he is supposed to leave. John tells him he needs to take a boat rather than a plane, because he just dreamt that the plane was going to crash. John then leaves because it's the end of his shift. The man listens to his bodyguard and takes a boat. Soon after arriving in Scotland, he hears that the plane he was supposed to take crashed. When he arrives home, he fires John. Why?

154.   Five mercenaries are sharing 12 diamonds. They decide to proceed that way. The one with the most experience will suggest a diamond allotment. The rest will vote for or against it. If the majority accepts, the sharing is ratified. If not, he will be dismissed. So, the sharing would be done between the remaining mercenaries with the same rules. Knowing that they are set from left to right in diminishing order of their experience, how would be the allotment?

155.   I can be solid or liquid; you can find me in any home, and sometimes, I bubble. What am I?

156.   How many hairs would you find in a rabbit's tail?

157.   I have no leaves, no trunk, no fruit, but I do have branches. What am I?

158.   According to the encyclopedia, which would come first? The chicken or the egg?

159.   I only come out at night, but I can't come out every night. I am not sleeping in the day, though many people think that I do. I'm always there; you're just not able to see me. Some people think I look like a bunny, while other people think I look like a person. I can look big or small. What am I?

160.   I come in second among a dozen, and I am very short. Every 4 years, I change in a way that none of the others do, which makes me unique and sets me apart. What am I?

161.   I am able to cycle for many hours, but I never get tired. Even at the end of the day, I can keep going. What am I?

162.   How many apples can you ingest if your abdomen is completely unoccupied?

163.   I do not have eyes, and I am completely white. Where I once had thoughts, I am now empty and hollow. What am I?

164.   I have the ability to be both hot and cold. I am able to run and be completely still. I can be rigid, or I

can be easy to mold. I can be high in volume, or I can be soft and more muted. Can you deduce what I am?

165. Which automobile is spelled the same way forward as it is backward?

166. I am cylindrical and long. I live in a house that can make you fall down, but I am easily crushed in the palm of your hand. I am nourishing and delicious. What am I?

167. I have 2 different cases, but I will never win or lose. I also will never have use for a lawyer. What am I?

168. I sit and wait with pointed fangs. I have a piercing force, and I can crunch out fates. I grab my victims with all my might, but I only physically join you with one single bite. Can you deduce what I am?

169. What kind of jacket will always be damp when you place it on your shoulders?

170. If you're in a dark cave and you only have one match, a single lump of coal, a kerosene lamp, and a stove, and you only have the option of lighting one, what would you light first to make sure that you're safe?

171. If I don't have this, then I'm already dead. If I am not dead, then I am already behind. Can you deduce what I am?

172. Can you guess what the moon and a single dollar bill have in common?

173. What has no other organs but 13 hearts?

174. What are 2 things you would never eat after just waking up?

175. If a rooster had laid a white and brown egg, what kind of chicks would hatch from the egg?

176. I am green, but I am not a lizard. I am white but without snow. I am bearded without being a man. What am I?

177. What always ends everything?

178. A biologist and a girl went shopping. The girl is the biologist's daughter, but the biologist is not her father. Who is the biologist?

179. What gets bigger, the more you take away from it?

180. I have two coins that will equal up to 30 cents. One of the coins is not a nickel. What are the 2 coins?

181. No gentlemen will possess me for their own, but I have the ability toencompass what they all need. I appear to be flat, but I am deep. Hidden realms, I

shelter. I can be calm, angry, and turbulent. Lives I take, but the food I offer. At times, I am beautiful. I have no heart, but I offer pleasure as well as death.

182.   What has only two words but hundreds of letters?

183.   How is Betty a half-century old in 1830, and yet 45 in 1835?

184.   There are 6 brothers. Each brother has 1 sister. How many sisters are in the brother's family?

185.   A container without a lock, key, or hinges, inside there is a prize of gold. What is it that I am?

186.   What is something that is unable to be burned or drowned in flames and water?

187.   What is half of 8? (It's not 4)

188.   What has green hair, a round head that is red, and a long, white beard that is very thin?

189.   I cause involuntary movements in the vehicle that you drive. What am I?

190.   What never walks that has a big mouth, is able to run but never talks?

191.   I am skilled at hiding what is real, and I am able to hide what is true. Sometimes, I can actually help you find the courage that resides deep inside of you. Can you deduce what I am?

192. If you immerse a stone into water, what will it become?

193. It's shorter than the rest, but you can raise it up like it's the best when you are happy. What is it?

194. I have two legs, but they only touch the ground when I am ready to rest. What am I?

195. I have a tongue, but I am never able to talk, andeven though I have no legs, I can sometimes walk. What am I?

196. I rarely get touched, but I am often held. If you are smart, you use me every day.

197. I have no legs to dance, nor lungs to sing. I dance to music all on my own and breathe with the same. What am I?

198. I am always in front of you, but you cannot see me. What am I?

199. When you lose me, you may make others lose theirs. What am I?

200. What is red but stops on green?

201. I am in a house and around it, but I never touch it. What am I?

202. I stand upright, and I am quite grand. I am elegant, and people like to look at me. I am right at your hands. What am I?

203. I can enchant anyone I see, and I can bring out the best in you. I can brighten someone's day, and I can sparkle and shine. What am I?

204. What has to take a bow before it can speak to you?

205. No man can ever see me, and no man ever will, but I will always be here. What am I?

206. I am a mother, and I support my children no matter what their weight. I can turn around without being called, and I have held use since the time you crawled. What am I?

207. What is harder and harder to catch the faster you run?

208. Two brothers run, but no matter how much they try, they cannot reach each other. What are they?

209. The roof is beneath, and the floor is on top. I rarely leave this place, and as each day passes, a new horizon greets my gaze. What am I?

210. What can pandas have that no other animal can have?

211. I live for 7 monthsand sing as the breeze whips by. I have many different colors. What am I?

212. I can turn and twist, and I leave a loop. What am I?

213.   Three men walk into a motel. The room they want is 30 dollars. Each guy pays ten dollars. Once they get to their room, the manager realizes that the room was only supposed to be 25 dollars. He sends an employee with five 1 dollar bills. On the way to the room, the employee thinks, "I can't split five 1s between 3 guys." So, he pockets 2 of the dollars and gives each of the men a dollar. Now, the men have only paid 9 dollars each. 9X3=27, and the employee pocketed 2 dollars, which makes 29. Where is the other dollar?

214.   An explorer is traveling to a prehistoric land. He sees a quartet of paths to follow. The foremost path has really deep mud. When people go there, they never come back. The second path has broken tracks, which is really unsafe for anyone who takes this path. On the third path, there is a lion who hasn't eaten and drunk anything for 3 months, so it is really hungry by now. The last path has dinosaurs and volcanoes, so it's a very dangerous place. Which path is the best one for the traveler to take?

215.   An old grandfather is making out his final will and testament and wishes to leave his belongings to one of his two kids—whoever is more dedicated. To

decide who will win his fortune, he gives them each a car and tells them that whoever's car passes the finish line last will get everything he owns.After a month of both kids refusing to cross the finish line, they finally go to their uncle for advice. They both leave their uncle's house in a hurry and race to the finish line as fast as they could. What did their uncle say to them?

216.   A father wishes to leave his valuables to a single child out of the trio he has sired, but he didn't know which one he should give it to. He gave each of them a few dollars and told them to go buy something that would fill their living room. The oldest son bought straws, but there was not enough to fill the room. The second son bought some sticks, but they still did not fill the room. The daughter bought two things that filled the room, so she obtained her father's fortune. What were the two things that the daughter bought?

217.   In certain societies, if a person has committed a misdeed that is grave, they will be shot at twice with a 6-bullet revolver. The revolver only has two bullets in it, though—both of them right next to each other. They spin the revolver once and shoot the gun. If there was no bullet in that chamber, they give the

person the option to either shoot again or spin the chamber again. If the first shot didn't shoot a bullet, then should the prisoner ask for the revolver to be spun, or should they choose that it be shot again?

218.   A duck is in the middle of a lake that is of a circle shape, but the duck is unable to take flight from the lake; only on land. Within the parameter of the lake, there is a hunting dog that desperately wants the duck, but cannot swim. So the duck must make it to the land before taking off, and must do so before the dog makes it to him. The dog is almost 4 times faster than the duck, and always runs to the point around the lake closest to the duck. How can the duck get out of the lake and take flight before the dog gets him?

219.   A store employee discovered a child that was lost.He is unable to speak, so he is unable to help the employee locate his parents. Three people came claiming they were the kid's parent. They are allowed to spend 2 minutes alone with the boy. The employee is watching them through the window. Parent 1: A woman with chocolate, a burger, and fries feeding the kid. Parent 2: "Where were you? I have been looking for you everywhere!?" Parent 3: "Look, it's your favorite car!" Who is the criminal?

220.   I have wisdom and knowledge beyond the ages. I get what you want in a split second. I am known to man as endless wisdom. What am I?

221.   What does a scientist call a dog?

222.   What is something that is always present but people can't see?

223.   If I turn my head, you will be able to go wherever it is you want to. If I turned again, you're going to be stuck, and you can rot. What am I?

224.   The faster the horse will run, the shorter his tail will become—an iron horse with a tail that is flaxen.

225.   I cry but have no eyes, I rejoice but have no heart. What am I?

226.   I can run, but I am unable to walk. What am I?

227.   I never sing till a shot fires out. What am I?

228.   I shed in one season and dress smartly for the next.

229.   I see you beneath me, and I hear your sights and sounds. Memories come with me, and emotions are strong. What am I?

230.   I get tagged with red or yellow stickers, and people come to me daily. What am I?

231. I can destroy kings and make them feeble. I can bring down towns and cities. What am I?

232. If you don't have me, the world will fall. Many people have one of me. What am I?

233. I can't be taken from you, but I am owned by all. What is it that I am?

234. I have only a duo of words, and yet I possess thousands of letters.

235. How many letters are in the alphabet?

236. You can hold me in your right hand but not the left. What am I?

237. I can be broken or read, watched, or live. What am I?

238. What starts as black, then turns red before finally turning white?

239. I have many colors, but you can't ever touch me.You may only see me.

240. I crack when you drop me. Even broken, I smile back.

241. My love for Eliza will never know my first, but it will not be my secondeither. Instead, it will be my whole.

242. What happens when your underwear attack you?

243. What can you add to water in a full bucket to make it lighter?

244. I have no tracks and no paths for you to tread. I am a field that stretches wide, and I shimmer like diamonds in the light.

245. For hundreds, I am their true wake up call.

246. I have no heart, just a body. I have a tongue but not a head. What am I?

247. I thunder with a breech and weigh more than a dozen men. What am I?

248. I rise on a pillar, and I can crawl all over the Earth but never stay for long. What am I?

249. You can find me where the sky has turned orange or where the blue oranges are present. Find me where the glass is red, or banana violets are present to your eyes.

250. I hold months and weeks, but I come in sizes big and small.

251. Slash me if you like, but I heal instantly.

252. Three heads I have got. Cut one; I am still stronger. Cut 2; I will rise and become 10.

253. I fly when I am born, and lay still when I am alive. I run as I die. What am I?

254. People see me without noticing I am there. I am beyond what you are seeking.

255. Feathers will give me the ability to take flight. Though I possess a body, I am not living; you determine how far I go. What am I?

256. Even if you don't kill me, I will die because when I live, I cry.

257. I have a big hump, and I spit, but I can take you where you need to get.

258. What hole can be mended with other holes?

259. Getting into me is simple. Getting out of me is difficult. Do you know what I am?

260. I point the way when I am filled. When I am empty, I am still. I have 2 skins. One within and one is without.

261. I travel from coast to coast and never move.

262. I live in the ground. I may not be much now, but I will be someday.

263. I only have one eye, but I see things better than those with two. I can save your memories and let you hold them dear.

264. Black within am I, and red without I am. I have 4 corners. What am I?

265. Through my wounds, you will see the water run. I once held many, but I have no more.

266. I walked for miles, and I finally got it. When I saw it, I threw it away, realizing I did not want it.

267. I am good and in a fine state. Unfortunately, those who are in are sadly out of it.

268. I can be repeated but only sometimes in the same way. I cannot be changed, but I have been rewritten. Don't forget me.

269. I come in many varieties and can bring harmony. You move when you hear me, but you can't physically touch me

270. I grow, but I am not alive. I am fun to have on hand when you're with your friends, and I love summertime.

271. I can fill your body, but you are unable to touch me.Death is something I can bring, but you can only see me.

272. If today is the one that appears prior to a couple of days after the one before tomorrow is the sixth day, then what day is it right now today?

273. I never swallow anything, but I have a hard bite. I go all over the hills, and I can make a pretty sight.

274.   What grows bigger and bigger the more you contract it?

275.   How many 9s are between the number one and the number 100?

276.   I am afraid of cats. I have two colors on my skin. I am always with my pack. What am I?

277.   I can help make you see or blind you. I can build a castle but not one that you can live in. What am I?

278.   I am a house. People walk in, and they are blind, but when people leave me, they can see. I've changed their life. What am I?

279.   A man and his boss, while having the same parents, are not related. How is this possible?

280.   I have a temper, and I blow my top when I do a make a mess of everything.

281.   I have 6 faces and 21 eyes. I have nobody to speak of, and I cannot see even with all these eyes that I have. What am I?

282.   I am one hole in one pole. I pack a hole that is the color of fresh milk. Every day, you will use me not as much as you did before, but much less so during the night. What am I?

283. It takes a good scholar to learn what I am. I am full of knowledge and have many words at hand.

284. I creep upon you slowly. I change shades, and I grow. I weep, and I weep, but do you know who I am?

285. Others have wrinkles as they get old, but I do not. The older I get, the fewer wrinkles I get.

286. What has teeth but doesn't possess a mouth?

287. Everyone has one of these. They are both hard and easy to keep.

288. My firstborn will study aerodynamics, while my next will be able to build many different engines. My next child is a skilled illustrator, and my last has the wisdom of an animal that is known for such. As for me? It's consistent with what you will tell. Are you able to find all of us?

289. Name a word with 7 letters, from which if you take out 4, you will have 1 left?

290. I add 5 to 9 and get 2. The answer is correct, but how?

291. Fred killed innocents and was responsible for $4.7 million for the damage he had caused.Although these facts are true, he was not made to pay anything. Why is this so?

292. There is one container without a lid, and had wine inside. "This container that holds the wine is more than half full," said Jack. Mike says, "No, it's not. It's less than half full." Without any measuring implements, and without removing any wine from the barrel, how can they figure out who is correct?

293. Six glasses placed in a line are being studied. The three that are at the start of the line are full of rum;the final three have nothing. If you are only able to move a single glass, can you place them so that the glasses alternate between rum and nothing?

294. Jack and Jill have been discovered to be deceased in a tiny spot of mud and liquid. There is broken glass scattered all around the mud.The building that housed the deceased bodies is next to the biggest train station. What happened to them that led them to die?

295. What is the only time it's ever okay to lock lips with a stranger if you're looking for encouragement to do so?

296. I grow with age, but you will need a lot of me to be what's known as a sage.

297. What is an age that most travelers have with them?

298.   What type of man is always above a board?

299.   Men love me, while women adore me. I am
never free. What am I?

300.   I burn and burn, and I never fall, but I am
made with glass walls.

Chapter Two: Answer Key

1. When there is a hole in it
2. A garbage truck
3. Eyes
4. A pig
5. A coffin
6. A candle
7. A piece of paper
8. A mushroom
9. A fire
10. You will stab me
11. A map
12. The letter "R"
13. Pencil lead
14. Your name
15. Water
16. The number seven consists of two syllables, while the others only contain one.
17. A fishhook
18. The letter "M"
19. Stand back to back to your mother.
20. My watch
21. To write and to read

22. A hyphen

23. White. It is a polar bear, because the only place you could hike that way and end up where you started is the North Pole. Polar bears are the only bears on that part of the Earth.

24. If I have daughters, then two statements are true. Therefore, I do not have any daughters at all.

25. We are pepper.

26. Brake/break

27. The buoy meeting the gull.

28. His son

29. The river was frozen.

30. Letter. It's the only one that doesn't make sense when you read it backward.

31. An hourglass, because of the grains of sand in it.

32. Short

33. Nine. There would be two parents, one daughter, and the six sons.

34. Nineteen

35. Meat

36. A penny

37. Neither. It's a coconut tree, and not a banana tree.

38. A pillow

39. You will need to fill the 3-cup container and then pour the 3 cups into the 5 cups. Repeat the process and fill the 5cups all the way, and what's left from the 3 cups would equal a single cup.

40. The group has a grandfather, father, and son.

41. A pencil

42. A shadow

43. A kangaroo

44. An egg

45. A teapot

46. Your breath

47. The moon

48. A glove

49. No one was lying. The three doctors were James' sisters.

50. A postman

51. A piano

52. A needle

53. No one would ever knock on their own hotel room door, and the man did.

54. Clouds

55. Cutlery and plates

56. Gum

57. The chef because he said he was making breakfast. Mr. Owens was killed in the afternoon, not in the morning.

58. Someone

59. A stamp

60. Fingerprints

61. Silence

62. The king had given each child a fake seed so that none of the plants would grow, and the little girl had been the only one honest enough to not switch the seeds to make herself look better.

63. She killed her sister because she wanted to see the man again, and she figured out that the only way she would be able to see him again was at her sister's funeral.

64. An address

65. The letter "W"

66. A secret

67. Eyes

68. A palm tree

69. Nothing

70. I am a joke.

71. A doorbell

72. A clock

73. I am a shadow.

74. I am a fish.

75. I am a traffic light. You beg the light to stay green as you approach.

76. Startling is the beginning word. When you remove the "l", it turns to "starting." From there, you will need to take away the "t" to turn the word into"staring." If you keep going from there, you can turn it into "sting," then "sing","sin","in", and then, finally, "I" when you've reached the final word.

77. The letter "E"

78. Time

79. A table

80. I am love.

81. A zipper

82. A leg

83. A kidney

84. Both men in this riddle were given drinks with poison. However, the poison was in the ice. Tommy had finished his drink at a rapid pace, and the ice was still intact. Because the ice stayed intact, the poison wasn't released, which is why he lived. Tony died because he was sipping his drink, and the ice had time to melt and release the poison that killed him.

85. Air

86. Fire

87. Get a package that is 9 feet on each of the sides and then place the sword diagonally in the box. It can be placed inside with plenty of room to spare. Therefore, it would not break any of the rules, and I would have it mailed to me on time.

88. Dark

89. I am a flight of stairs.

90. A waterfall. While the water runs, the waterfall remains still because it never moves or changes location.

91. Your posture

92. A knife

93. A toilet

94. The driver wasn't driving. He was walking. Therefore, no crime was committed.

95. Only ten

96. An echo

97. He was cleaning windows on the inside, not the outside.

98. A wedding ring

99. A foot. The "twin" is the other foot.

100.   The only flies that are remaining on a table are the 10 that you killed. The others would naturally fly away when you started swatting.

101.   The reason that the principle is confused is that the student has double-counted a lot of his days. So his math, while smart, is potentially incorrect in many ways. A lot of the time that he would be sleeping or relaxing occurs during the weekends and during the summer. Weekends occur during the summer and during the year, so his calculations were getting counted more times than they needed to be counted. Instead of counting them once, he was counting them several times. Another thing that he forgot is that school does not last all day. Schools in many countries only last for 6 or 8 hours per day, which means you have the rest of the day to do whatever it is that you would need to do. In that case, the 4 days that he was actually calculating for school would be 16 days or more: If his school was 6 hours per day, those 4 days would only represent 16 days of school. So the principle is confused because the student's calculation of time was wrong.

102.   They all had red gloves. There were only 3 possible combinations, and we knew that they

couldn't all have yellow gloves because the king had already said at least one of them had a red glove, so from there, you can start the process of elimination and learn that they would be able to identify that they all had a red glove.

103.   They were able to deduce that Kyle was not telling the truth because the man was stabbed in the chest. When Kyle was interviewed by the police, he had said that the man was stabbed from behind.

104.   The thief was Paige. Bonnie was telling the truth when she said she did not steal it, and Heather was lying, so she says the Bonnie didn't do it either to reinforce that fact. Paige was lying, so she did it.

105.   On the twelfth night, she will wear blue again.

106.   The reason that Stewart dies is that when he deduced he was about to lose, he found out that the only way he could live was to replace his poison with something that isn't poison at all, and then he would need to drink the poison of his own before the contest. In this way, he would be drinking his weaker poison and neutralizing it with Lenny's stronger poison. So he drinks the non-poison that he submitted to the contest of the best poison maker. Once Lenny realized that this was the only way that Stewart could save

himself, he figures out that he would be able to save himself by either drinking a poison that is weaker before the contest so that his poison would neutralize it during the contest itself or submit a poison that is a non-poison to the contest like Stewart did. If he were drinking the weaker poison before the contest, they would both live, and the king would realize that they were disobeying his orders; they could both either be exiled or killed. But by submitting a poison that is not a poison to the contest, Stewart would end up drinking the weaker poison before the contest and that the two non-poisons that they submitted to the contest would still make him die, but the king would be none the wiser, but he still would not get what he wanted because the two poisons were not poison at all.

107.　　You should choose the first door and sit in the seat. Because there is no power, when you are in the seat, it is not going to have any effect on you or your body when the other rooms would.

108.　　The only way that you would be able to survive is to eat half of every pill. Your grandfather gave you 2 pink pills and 2 green pills. So if you split each pill in half, then it won't matter that you can't see them because half of 4 pills is 2 pills.

109.   I am musical notes.

110.   The reason that they went to the bad barbershop is that the clean-cut barber with the immaculate hair has his hair styled by the unkempt stylist, and the unkempt stylist has his haircut done by the clean-cut stylist. This is made obvious as they are the only 2 barbers in town, and by that approximation, it's obvious that the dirty barber would be the barber who gives a better haircut.

111.   The cells that would still be open are 1,4, 9, 16, 25, 36, 49, 64, 81, and, of course, the 100th cell. Only the cells that have 2 of the same factors would be open because they are opened and closed the same number of times. Because they have the same factor twice, this makes their number of factors odd.

112.   The police knew about the robbery because when the teller was talking to her mother, she used the mute button on the phone, so the only words her mother actually heard her say were "emergency,""call," and the word "help." The teller's mother immediately called the police and told the

police that there was a problem at the bank, which led the police to go to the bank to see what was wrong.

113.   What he should ask is the question: "Is she older than her?" and when he asks this, he should always pick the younger daughter based on what he knows. If he asked the older daughter this question, and she had said yes, then he would know who the youngest daughter is because the older daughter always tells the truth. If he asks and she says "no," then the youngest daughter is the other one. If he had asked his questions to the younger daughter, and she says "yes," then he already knows that she's lying, and he would pick the oldest instead. If he had asked the youngest, and she said "no," then he would pick the other one like in the first case because you would know that she's still lying. However, if he asked the middle daughter, it wouldn't matter because both would be acceptable choices.

114.   At the beginning of the story, it was said that the day was windless. In the end, it said the flag was waving back and forth. Because it was windless, the flag would have been completely still, and it wouldn't have been able to move. The only way it could have

moved is if somebody was forcing it to move back and forth.

115.   The answer is that Johnny already had one cat, so when she asked him how many,he would have 7 if he was given 6, because 6 + 1 is 7.

116.   He was the most powerful and then not anymore. If you read the first sentence of this riddle again, it states that he *was* the strongest man in the world. Saying the word "was" is past tense, which means that someone is stronger than him now, which is why he placed second and not first.

117.   She would need 16 apples.

118.   The third man. The third man understands the color of his own hat as he deduced that there is only a duo of each of the colored hats. The man placed behind him saw a duo of hats that were the same in front of his vision, then he knows that his hat must be the other color. We are able to see that because of the alternating colors, the last man only has half of the odds of getting his own right. So the last man stays silent. The third understands why the last man is silent and deduces that he cannot view a duo that matches in front of his eyes. If he could, he would speak, but he hasn't. So the third man is able to

presume his own hat must be a different color than the one in front of him, and his presumption is correct in this case. Under that same logic, after the third man tells the color of his hat, the second man, even though he only sees the wall, would be able to go free next because he knows his hat would be the opposite of whatever color the third man's hat was.

119.   The prisoners would have to choose a leader, and then everyone else would need to be a follower. If you are a follower, then you would need to make sure that switch A is in the on position and toggle switch B. Then you would not have been able to toggle switch A, and you would have been able to see the switch on during a previous visit. Then, you should toggle switch A. Instead, you would toggle switch B if you were the leader.Then you would need to turn switch A on. If it was off, turn switch A on. If it was on, and you did not turn on switch A during the previous visit, then you would need to increment the count of prisoners. Once the leader had incremented the count to 23, they would be able to yell that every prisoner has been here. Then all of them would be released because they would be correct.

120.   You would walk to the left and drink the fourth
    and the third. There would be no point in going to the
    right, because there are only 2 test tubes on the right,
    and the iguana poison is going to override the
    antidote to the other poison. The cow is number 2,
    which means that the iguana is either in number one
    or number 4. If the cow is number 2, then that would
    mean that the lizard is number 1, 2, or 3. Since we
    have been able to deduce that the iguana is either 1 or
    4, the iguana and the lizard cannot be beside each
    other, and we know that the cow is number 2. That
    makes it impossible for the iguana's saliva to be 3 or 4.
    Using what we know, now that we understand the
    iguana's number,we drink 3 and 4 because the lizard
    would be in either 3 or 4, and you would be safe from
    the poison.

121.   One would allow a single person to flip the bulb
    off. The rest would turn it on if they had never turned
    it on before. If they have turned it on before, then,
    they will do nothing. The prisoner who can turn it off
    then knows that they have all been there, and he could
    save them all when he turns it off 99 times.

122.   The pain was transferred to the man who sired
    the infant. The mother had been unfaithful with the

mailman. It was the mailman's baby. It never mentions that the husband is the baby's father, but because the mailman is dead on the porch, we can deduce that he was the baby's father and that the pain killed him.

123. The German

124. Brandon brings his sleeping bag home when he realizes he forgot his flashlight. He leaves his sleeping bag at home. He realized he did not bring his tent; Brandon then goes home with his flashlight. Instead of picking up his tent, he sees his sleeping bag and takes that instead, leaving his tent and flashlight at home. He goes back when he gets to camp because he now needs his flashlight and tent. Brandon brings his sleeping bag,and when he gets his tent and flashlight, he leaves his sleeping bag. Every time he brings something to the campsite, he leaves what he had at home.

125. Before they entered the bar, the gentleman with the baseball cap told the cowboy, "If I can spray beer everywhere in the bar and make the bartender laugh, you have to give me five thousand dollars."

126. Mike can figure it out. If Josh saw that Mike and Brad had their hats are in the same color, he

would know his hat color. Since he doesn't quickly figure out his hat color, Mike knows that his hat and Brad's don't have the same hat color. So all he has to do is say that his hat color is the opposite of Brad's hat color (after giving enough time to be sure that Josh doesn't know his own color).

127.   I am a bad conductor.

128.   Imagine thatonly one resident lives on the island. He will look to see that there are no green-eyed residents, and once this happens, he would realize that he knows his eye color. If there are 2, they will see that there is one person with one color, and if the person did not leave,it means that they would have the same eye color. The same logic is true for the other person's viewpoint. With this knowledge, the green-eyed people would be able to leave in a certain number of days because each resident will need an additional day to know what color they have.

129.   Water, earth, air, fire, and spirit.

130.   He lost $5. The woman from the thrift shop gave him $20 in change but eventually got $20 back. She broke even. The guy who spent 15 dollars gave the manager nothing (except counterfeit money) but got

$5 back from the manager. So the manager lost only $5 and gave free products.

131.   The woman didn't look at the entrance. She knew her husband wouldn't come in.

132.   The individual with the canine photo. The other duo had voted the other's post down and their own up. The canine photo owner voted each person's up.

133.   The criminal set up all the guards so that each person is directly across the other. If they fired, they would possibly shoot the other guards so they couldn't shoot at all.

134.   The hat is orange. If Jack doesn't know the color of his hat, then the other two men's hats cannot both be red; otherwise, he would know that his hat is orange. When James doesn't know his hat color either, that means Jim's hat could not be red; otherwise, Jack would have to know his hat was orange to fulfill the information discovered through Jack's answer.

135.   They figured out that they needed 5 people to make the plan work.One person is in each corner, and one person needs to be moving at all times from one

to the other. This means there is someone else in the building already.

136.   One answer is the following. Ask the second man, "If I were going to ask if you are Random, would you say 'ja'?" If 2 answers "ja", either 2 is Random (and is answering randomly), or 2 is not Random, and the answer indicates that 1 is indeed Random. Either way, 3 is not Random. If 2 answers "da", either 2 is Random (and is answering randomly), or 2 is not Random, and the answer indicates that 1 is not Random. Either way, you know the identity of a guy who is not Random. Q2: Go to the guy who was identified as not being Random by the previous question (either 1 or 2), and ask him, "If I asked you 'Are you False?', would you say 'ja'?" Since he is not Random, an answer of "da" indicates that he is True, and an answer of "ja" indicates that he is False. Q3: Ask the same guy the question: "If I asked you, 'Is 2 Random?', would you say 'ja'?" If the answer is "ja", 2 is Random; if the answer is da, the guy you have not yet spoken to is Random. The remaining guy can be identified by elimination.

137.   It could be any word as long as it contained a quintet of letters. In each of the examples, the guard

had said something, and then the person responded with something different. But the word they said had a single letter more than the word that the guard had said first.

138.   Each of the husbands who are unfaithful will be murdered, and it will take one less night than the number of cheating husbands for their wives to discover this. If one man was cheating, and that woman hadn't have heard of any other infidelity, she would know it was her husband who was cheating. If two husbands are cheating, both of their wives would think that since they have only heard of one man cheating, he should die the next morning. If he doesn't die, she knows her husband must also be cheating, and that's the reason the other husband didn't die. Following this logic, you know that all of the men will die after one less night than there are cheating men.

139.   The black criminal will yell "black" if there is an uneven number of black shirts in front of him and "white" if there is an even number of black shirts in front of him. The next criminal will then count the number of black shirts in front of him, and if it was odd and is now even, or vice versa, then that person knows what color their shirt is. The next person then

knows their shirt color based on what the people before them said and how many black shirts are in front of them. In this way, the front 99 criminals will know their shirt color and will be set free. The criminal in the back who goes first has a 50 percent chance of being set free.

140.   He sang the song "Happy Birthday" because any name can be put into it. The rich woman honored the deal, so he went home rich.

141.   His horse was named "Friday".

142.   It's an electric train; there's no smoke.

143.   The letter M

144.   A heart

145.   A gymnast

146.   A keyboard for a computer

147.   Chocolate

148.   An ant

149.   The alphabet

150.   First, Jack and Jason will cross the wire (in a duo of minutes). Then Jack brings the flashlight back (1 minute). Next, Alex and Cindy will cross (10 minutes). Then Jason will bring the flashlight back (2 minutes). And finally, Jason and Jack will cross (2 minutes). 2 + 1 + 10 + 2 + 2 = 17 minutes.

151.   His sons are 8, and the last two are 3 years of age. The prime factorization of 72 is 2 * 2 * 2 * 3 * 3, so the possible ages are 2, 3, 4, 6, 8, 9, 12, and 18. Using that knowledge again, and these numbers, the only combinations of numbers that would be able to work for the first clue are 18, 2, and 2; 9, 4, and 2; 6, 6, and 2; 6, 4, and 3; and 8, 3, and 3. Since she doesn't know the ages after this piece of information, the sum of the three numbers must not be unique. The sum of 8, 3, and 3 and 6, 6, and 2 are the same. Now, the final clue comes in handy. Since we know that the oldest son has his own bed, it is likely that he has the bed to himself, and is older than the other two, so their ages are 8, 3, and 3 rather than 2, 6, and 6.

152.   The outdated password is "out of date," and the current password is "different."

153.   John was sleeping on the job.

154.   9-0-1-0-2.

155.   I am soap.

156.   You'd find none as they're all outside.

157.   A bank

158.   The chicken, because the encyclopedia always goes in alphabetical order, of course.

159.   The moon

160. February

161. A clock

162. Only one. After that, your stomach will not be empty.

163. A skull

164. Water

165. A racecar

166. A banana

167. Letters, both uppercase and lowercase. This makes the two cases.

168. A stapler

169. A coat of paint

170. You would light the match first.

171. Ahead

172. 4 quarters

173. A deck of cards

174. Lunch and dinner

175. None. Roosters can't lay eggs.

176. A leek

177. The letter "G", because it's at the end of everything.

178. The girl's mother.

179. A hole

180. It's a trick question. One of the coins is not a nickel, but the other one is. So the answer is a nickel and a quarter.

181. Ocean

182. Post office

183. She was born in 1880 B.C.

184. 1 sister. If there were 6 sisters, each brother would have had 6 sisters

185. An egg

186. Ice. It is capable of avoiding burning in flames as it melts instead, but it floats in liquid.

187. 3 (if you cut it in a vertical manner). 0 (if you cut in a horizontal manner).

188. A radish

189. A tow truck

190. A river

191. Makeup

192. Whetstone

193. A thumb

194. Wheelbarrow

195. A shoe

196. Tongue

197. A flame

198. Your future

199. Your temper

200. A watermelon

201. The sun

202. A piano

203. A smile

204. A violin

205. Tomorrow

206. The Earth

207. Your breath

208. Wheels

209. A sailor

210. A family of baby pandas

211. A leaf

212. A shoelace

213. There is no lost dollar: The order of operation was not followed. The employee still had 5 dollars to bring to the men.

214. He should walk down the path with the lion. Having been deprived of food for three months, it would have succumbed to starvation and would be unable to kill him.

215. Their uncle told the two kids to drive each other's car. If one drives the other's car past the winner's line, their car will be last, and they will win.

216.   The smart daughter had purchased a box that contained matches and a candle. After making sure that the candle was lit properly, the light from the candle filled the room entirely.

217.   They should have them shoot it again. There is a 2/6 chance they will get shot if it's spun again. There are four possible spots that don't have bullets, and only one is followed by a bullet. This means that if they don't spin it, there is a 1/4 chance that they will be shot.

218.   The duck can travel a quarter of the journey to land before swimming in a circular path around the center of the lake (the duck will be moving slightly faster around than the dog in their circles). Once the duck is as far as he can get away from the dog in his circle, he can swim the remaining 3/4 of the way to shore. The dog must travel the radius of the lake times Pi (radius * π) while the duck only has to travel 3/4 the radius four times slower (3/4 * radius * 4). So the duck will be able to make it to the shore and fly before the dog reaches it.

219.   Parent 1: Who would give that so much junk food to a child that was unable to speak and who was

small? And, parent 3: This is a ploy of kidnappers. They offer toys.

220.	Computer
221.	A canine
222.	Noise
223.	Key
224.	A needle
225.	A cloud
226.	A nose
227.	A gun
228.	A tree
229.	The past
230.	The clearance section
231.	Time
232.	An atlas
233.	Knowledge
234.	The post office
235.	11. The two words, "The" and "alphabet".
236.	Your left hand
237.	The news
238.	Charcoal
239.	A rainbow
240.	A mirror
241.	Endless

242.   You have a wedgie.

243.   A hole

244.   The ocean

245.   Coffee

246.   A bell

247.   A cannon

248.   A shadow

249.   Negative

250.   A calendar

251.   Water

252.   A fox

253.   Snow

254.   A window

255.   An arrow

256.   A candle

257.   A camel

258.   A net

259.   Trouble

260.   Gloves

261.   A highway

262.   A seed

263.   Camera

264.   A chimney

265.   A shipwreck

266.   A thorn

267.   Sane

268.   History

269.   Music

270.   Marshmallow

271.   Smoke

272.   Friday

273.   Frost

274.   Debt

275.   20

276.   A zebra

277.   Sand

278.   A church

279.   He is self-employed. He is his own boss.

280.   A volcano

281.   Dice

282.   An eye

283.   A book

284.   Spring

285.   Tires

286.   A saw

287.   Secrets

288.   A E I O U (vowels)

289.   Someone

290. When it is 9:00 am, add 5 hours to it, and you will get 2:00 pm.

291. Fred was a hurricane!

292. Tilt the container until the wine barely touches the lip. If the bottom is visible, then it is less than half full. If the barrel bottom is still completely coveredbecause of the liquid, then it is more than half full.

293. Move and then pour all the liquid from glass number two to glass number five.

294. Jack and Jill are fish. A passing train rattled the shelf their tank was sitting on and knocked it off the shelf. The tank broke, and the fish died from being out of the water.

295. When performing CPR

296. Wisdom

297. Baggage

298. A chessman

299. Gold

300. A lantern

Conclusion

In this book, you have found 300 medium-to-hard riddles that were designed to stimulate your brain into thinking of solutions, thereby exercising it and improving its cognitive function. This book also serves to help you improve your memory. The riddles in this book have been written from varying degrees, so that no matter what your skill level is when it comes to problem-solving, you will be able to come with the right answer or get some practice in. If you have not arrived at the correct answer, that is perfectly fine. Everyone is at a different skill level when they begin to attempt riddles such as these, which is the reason that we have mixed them up so that they are not all complicated.

These riddles are designed to challenge you, improving your cognitive function, and helping your interpersonal skills get better and become more efficient. The best part about reading this book, however, is that your memory will improve, and as you get older, you won't have to worry about becoming less competent, because your brain will be sharp and clear. Knowing that you are helping your brain in the best way possible is both satisfying and rewarding when you let yourself have fun and do something worthwhile at the same time.

We have given you the tools in this book, which will help you actively exercise your brain that will be beneficial to you in the long run. Many people engage in things that make their body or spirit better, but we must remember that our mental health needs love and care as well.

Most of the activities that people do for their brain can be overtasking, and for others, it can seem like a chore. This is one of the reasons that college students feel over-pressured and burned out. Adults feel this way, too, especially when they have too much work to do. The things that stress us become a chore that we do over and over. Once we get to that point, things become less fun; even tools like riddles and puzzles become less interesting because your mind is already overworked. These riddles, however, are designed to be fun and engaging. You will find that you'd like to solve them because they do not feel boring; they are not like a menial task that you would rather avoid.

What's most interesting about the riddles that you will see in this book is that everyone can come up with the same answer, or a different one. No matter how you solve these riddles and puzzles, they will all help you understand yourself better. They will help you understand the way you think better, especially if you keep on reading this book and practicing your skills with riddles and puzzles. This book will also help you reflect on yourself. Many times, we can understand who we are, but we may not understand everything, such as how complex our minds are.

This book will help you understand the way you think and what your mind is capable of. The results may surprise you when you begin to do these riddles on a daily basis.

Connect with us on our Facebook page

www.facebook.com/bluesourceandfriends and stay tuned to our

latest book promotions and free giveaways.

Printed in Great Britain
by Amazon

10027491R00068